Ann Gianola

A Viral
Disturbance

DELTA Publishing

You can listen to *A Viral Disturbance* using the free DELTA Augmented app – you'll also find fun interactive activities!

| Download the free DELTA Augmented app onto your device | Start picture recognition and scan the **contents page** | Download files and use them now or save them for later |

Apple and the Apple logo are trademarks of Apple Inc., registered in the US and other countries. App Store is a service mark of Apple Inc. | Google Play and the Google Play logo are trademarks of Google Inc.

Photos: **4** Shutterstock (MiaMilky), New York; **6** Shutterstock (MaxterDesign), New York; **76** Shutterstock (VanReeel), New York; **79** Shutterstock (PHCZ), New York; **83** Shutterstock (Paranyu), New York; **83** Shutterstock (Pand P Studio), New York; **88** Shutterstock (PEAPIZA), New York; **89** Shutterstock (Inspiring), New York; **89** Shutterstock (Limolida Design Studio), New York; **90** Shutterstock (robuart), New York

1st edition 1 ⁵ ⁴ ³ ² ¹ | 2025 24 23 22 21

Delta Publishing, 2021
www.deltapublishing.co.uk

© Ernst Klett Sprachen GmbH, Rotebühlstraße 77, 70178 Stuttgart, 2021

Authors:
Text: Ann Gianola
Annotations and activities: Bernardo Morales

Cover and layout: Andreas Drabarek
Illustrations: Harald Ardeias
Typesetting: Datagroup Int. SRL, Timisoara, Romania
Cover picture: Harald Ardeias
Printing and binding: Salzland Druck, Staßfurt, Germany

ISBN 978-3-12-501134-2

Contents

Abbreviations

sth   = something
sb   = somebody

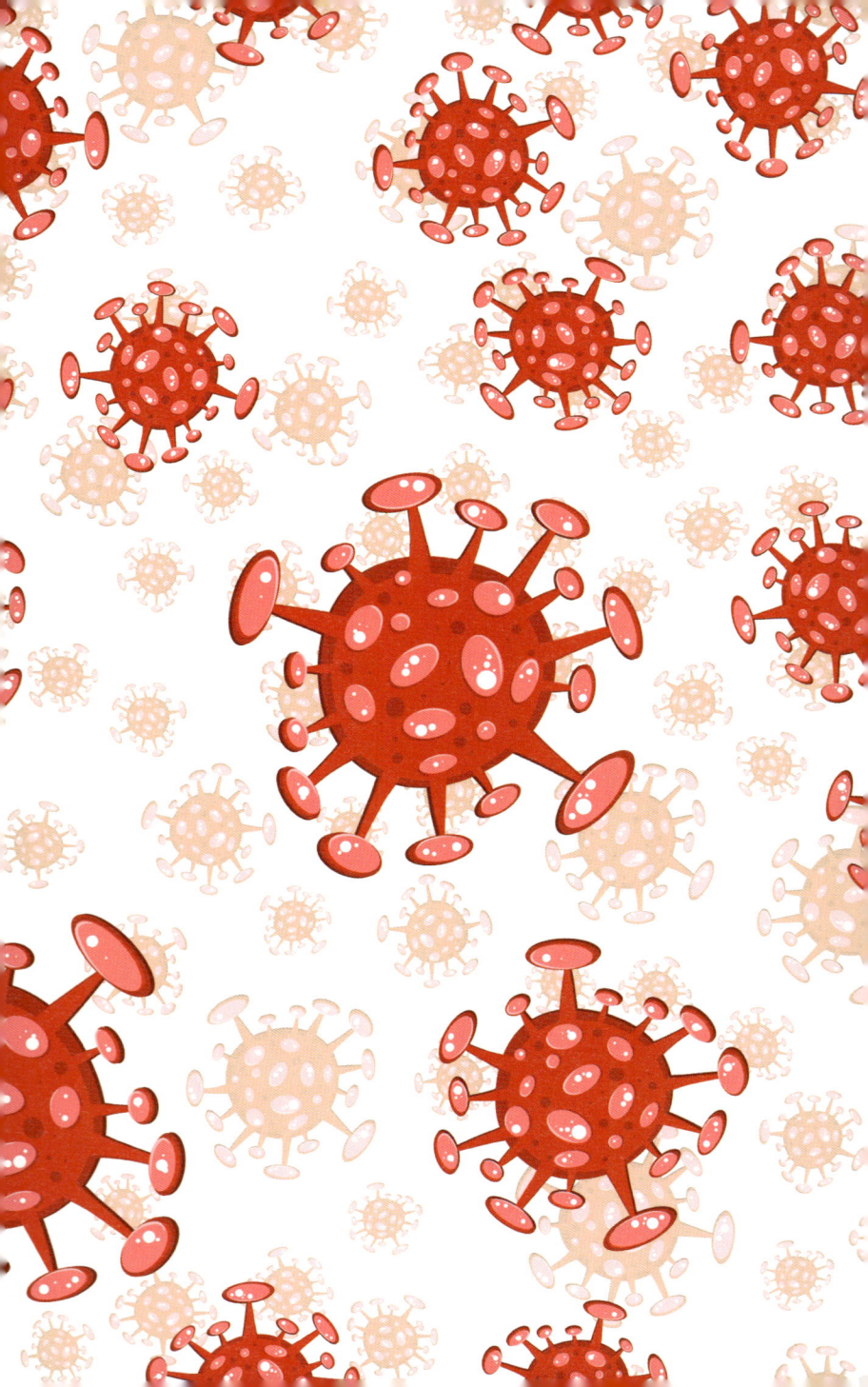

Before you start

1. Look at the illustrations of the main characters in the story.
    Think of three adjectives to describe the characters based on how
    they look. As you read the story, check to see if you were right,
    and make changes as you find out more about them.

Oscar   Mari

Clara   Emma

2. What does the American dream mean to you? Finish these sentences.

The American dream is…

In order to achieve the American dream you have to…

3. Clara's professor claims that the American dream is now over. Do you agree?

4. Look at the cover and the illustrations below. What do you think the story is about?

5. Read the story. Were you right?

Chapter 1

Oscar looked around his Mexican restaurant. Then he pressed his hands together and smiled. Every table was occupied. There was a long line of people at the door. He heard Mari, his wife, talking to a customer on the phone. "Right now, the wait for a table is about an hour," she said politely. "It's very busy tonight."

Mariachis played and sang in the large, colorful dining room. Servers carefully carried hot plates of *tacos*, *enchiladas*, and *tamales*. Hungry patrons were delighted. "Oh, this looks delicious!" said Linda, a weekly regular, picking up her fork. "Oscar's has the best Mexican food in the world!" Everyone at her table agreed. Oscar felt proud. "I've arrived," he thought with satisfaction. "This is the American dream… and I am really living it!"

Thirty years ago, Oscar was an eighteen-year-old immigrant from Mexico. At adult school in Southern California, his English

---

19 **to occupy** to be taken – 25 **patron** a restaurant customer – 25 **delighted** very happy – 28 **proud** feeling of satisfaction when you have done something good – 30 **immigrant** sb who has come from another country to live in a new country

---

teacher talked about the American dream. She believed that *anyone* – regardless of birthplace or class – could be successful in the U.S. "You can live the American dream," she declared, "if you work hard." At the time, Oscar was doubtful.

"But I am working hard," he thought, looking at his hands, red and rough from washing dishes at a Korean restaurant. Naturally, Oscar wanted to believe his teacher. And his main goal, like many other immigrants, was success. Still, it was difficult to imagine being truly successful. Reality was standing in front of a mountain of dishes and earning only minimum wage. At that time, his daily goal was survival.

At school, Oscar remembered writing something in his notebook. Using the present and past tenses, he wrote two positive sentences: "Today, I *wash* dishes. Yesterday, I *washed* dishes." Then, in the future tense, he wrote a negative one: "Tomorrow, I *won't wash* dishes." Oscar didn't mean *tomorrow* as the very next day. In fact, he washed dishes at the Korean restaurant for eight more months. He meant it as a promise to himself. He wouldn't stay at the bottom of the ladder forever. Tomorrow – whenever tomorrow was – there were more opportunities.

In time, Oscar's English improved a lot. He found better jobs in other restaurants, and he never washed dishes again. In some places, Oscar cooked in the kitchens. In others, he worked as a busboy, server, or cashier. Later, he became a manager. After working at restaurants for twenty years, he knew the business inside out. So, ten years ago, he got a business loan and opened his own Mexican restaurant – Oscar's – on Fourth Avenue.

Since Oscar's first opened, the business tripled in size. It now employed twenty-five people, plus four *mariachi* players. "I pinch

---

2 **regardless of** not depending on – 6 **rough** not soft, usually from working hard – 19 **the bottom of the ladder** the lowest position in a company – 22 **to improve** to get better – 26 **to know sth inside out** to be very familiar with sth – 27 **business loan** money from the bank to use to start a business – 30 **Mariachi** a traditional Mexican type of music

myself sometimes," Oscar said, walking toward Mari. "I'm afraid that I'll wake up… and be washing dishes again at the Korean restaurant."

"It is incredible," Mari replied, patting her husband's shoulder affectionately. "And I hope business stays this way," she added. "Next year, we'll have *two* daughters in college. It will cost a fortune."

"Don't worry about the money," answered Oscar, counting at least twenty people on Mari's waiting list. "It's a drop in the bucket. We worked hard and became successful. We're living the American dream."

How would you describe Oscar's restaurant?

How did Oscar achieve his dream of owning a restaurant?

Think about it…

Have you ever eaten at a Mexican restaurant? What did you eat? Would you go again?

In this chapter Oscar talks about the American dream. What is the American dream?

4 **to pat** to touch sb gently with the palm of your hand – 5 **affectionately** in a way that shows love – 6 **to cost a fortune** to be very expensive – 9 **a drop in the bucket** sth is small or insignificant

Chapter 2

Oscar and Mari had two daughters: Clara and Emma. Clara, twenty years old, was in her third year at a well-known university. Emma, three years younger, was in her last semester of high school. She had already been accepted to an excellent college and planned to start in the fall. Mari was right. Their schools would cost a fortune next year. But, thanks to the restaurant, Oscar and Mari could afford it. They were happy to support Clara's dream to become a dentist and Emma's to become a software engineer. Of course, this meant many years of expensive higher education. But money was no object. They had more than enough – and could handle the expense.

Clara and Emma grew up at Oscar's restaurant. When they weren't studying, they often worked there. As children in elementary school, they cleaned tables, swept floors, and wiped off plastic menus. Later, Clara and Emma helped out in the kitchen, sometimes washing dishes. Like their father, it wasn't a job they particularly enjoyed. "Yet, it's good for you," said Oscar, handing them two pairs of rubber gloves and pointing toward the sink. "Believe me, *big* dreams begin by scrubbing pots and pans."

Oscar regularly reminded his daughters that he was a living example of the American dream. "I started with nothing here – absolutely nothing. And look at me now!" he said proudly, putting a hand on his chest. "I've gone from rags to riches!" Clara and Emma were impressed by the efforts of both their parents, neither born into wealth. In comparison, their lives were quite privileged: a nice home, good schools, and no real worries about money. Washing dishes wasn't necessarily about survival. It also "built character," according to their father. So, when asked, the girls put on their rubber gloves and did the job.

---

5 **fall** (*American English*) autumn – 10 **money is no object** the price of sth is no reason to worry – 11 **expense** cost – 14 **to wipe off** to remove sth, such as pieces of food, from sth – 18 **to hand sb sth** to give sb sth – 29 **rubber** elastic, stretchy material

*****

It was a Saturday evening in January. Clara had recently returned to her university after the holidays, and Oscar, Mari and Emma were working in the restaurant. "Thanks for your help," said Mari, smiling at her daughter. "You can see that we're busy here – and unfortunately short-staffed at the moment."

"I can see that," said Emma, putting an apron over her head.

"Would you please bus tables tonight?" asked Mari. "Poor Luz is doing the whole dining room by herself." Emma quickly joined Luz and began clearing tables.

"I can't believe you're the only busser," said Emma. "Where is everyone?"

"Juan isn't back from Mexico yet," said Luz. "And Pedro is really sick," she said quietly, setting down clean placemats, napkins and silverware at a four-person table. "I guess it's some type of flu."

"I'm sorry to hear that," Emma replied. "Ugh. The flu. That's awful."

"It certainly is," said Luz. "There are some terrible germs going around right now. We have to be very careful – especially in jobs like ours." Emma moved to the next table, quickly gathering up dirty glasses and crumpled napkins. "Remember to wash your hands a lot," Luz advised. "And try not to touch your face."

"Thanks for reminding me," said Emma, resisting a sudden urge to scratch her nose. "You're right. Terrible, *terrible* germs going around."

---

6 **short-staffed** with fewer people working than usual – 7 **apron** a piece of cloth, usually tied around your waist, that is used to protect your clothes from getting dirty when cooking – 8 **to bus a table** to clean a table after a customer has left – 11 **busser** sb who cleans tables at a restaurant – 14 **placemat** material placed under a plate to protect the table from the heat of the food – 15 **silverware** knives, forks and spoons – 18 **germs** micro-organisms that can transmit a disease

Why does Oscar think that washing dishes at the restaurant is good for his daughters?

Why does Luz advise Emma to wash her hands?

Think about it ...

Clara wants to become a dentist. What would you like to study?

Clara and Emma work at their parents' restaurant in their free time. Have you ever had a summer job? What did you do?

Chapter 3

On Sunday afternoon, Oscar and Mari were at home, getting ready to leave for the restaurant. They had already packed three big boxes of cleaning supplies. Emma came down the stairs, her dark hair pulled up into a bun, wearing a white blouse and black pants. She was going to bus tables again. "What's all this?" Emma asked, looking at the boxes.

"We're trying to keep Oscar's extra clean," answered Mari. "You know, paying more attention – now."

"Good idea," said Emma, examining the containers of disinfecting wipes. "I mean, can you believe what's happening in Wuhan, China?" she asked. "People are dying from this horrible illness – the one caused by the *novel coronavirus*!" Oscar waved his hands irritably. He didn't want to hear any more.

3 **cleaning supplies** cleaning materials – 9 **container** sth you can store things in –
10 **disinfecting wipes** soft tissues you can use to clean things

"Yes, that's bad news… and I agree that we need our business to be as clean as possible," said Oscar, sighing with annoyance. "But, at the moment, I can't worry about what's happening across the world. We need to get to the restaurant now. Emma, can you please carry one of these boxes to the car?"

Inside the car, Oscar, Mari, and Emma rode for a while in silence. Emma looked out the window, admiring the view of the ocean from the top of the hill. It was a beautiful view, and usually Oscar was excited by it. Today, however, he was in no mood to talk about the ocean, the pretty hillside, and the eucalyptus trees. The scenery was not on his mind at all. He didn't want to admit it, but he was worried about the virus.

Mari turned on the radio. A news reporter announced a lockdown in Wuhan, a city of more than 11 million people. To help control the spread of the disease, people needed to stay home. Planes and trains couldn't leave the city. Oscar tried to turn off the radio, but Mari stopped him. "Furthermore," the voice continued, "there are new cases in Taiwan, Japan, Thailand, South Korea, and the United States."

"Oh, no!" cried Emma. "It's *here*! I wonder if Pedro has it – I mean, it's possible that his flu is actually the…" Oscar groaned loudly.

"Emma, stop!" he pleaded, "I'm sure that Pedro has something else. There are many viruses in the world. Please, let's not listen to this! It isn't useful."

Mari turned off the radio. Emma, however, had to speak up. "But it is useful, *Papi*," she said. "The world is very small now. And we're all connected. This virus affects everyone. We need to know the facts."

---

10 **hillside** landscape with hills – 11 **scenery** natural landscape – 14 **lockdown** a government measure where people are asked not to leave their homes – 15 **spread** distribution – 15 **disease** illness – 21 **to groan** to make a sound that expresses pain or frustration

"Fine," said Oscar. "Then read about the facts – if you really need to know more. But I need to manage a busy restaurant tonight. I need to feel calm – not upset! Can you please understand that?"

That night, the crowd was smaller at the restaurant. And Oscar felt the difference. He hoped that the news wasn't already hurting business. At 7:00, a man walked inside the restaurant. Oscar gave him a big smile. "*Buenas noches*, Nick!" Oscar said, warmly greeting his longtime customer.

"Hey, Oscar!" responded Nick. "Nice to see you."

"You too," said Oscar sincerely. "The *tamales* are fantastic tonight. I know how much you like them."

"You didn't add the *coronavirus* to your recipe, did you?" asked Nick, laughing loudly at his own bad joke. Oscar pretended that he hadn't heard him… because that joke wasn't funny whatsoever.

> Why did Emma try to keep the restaurant extra clean?

> Why was Oscar so quiet in the car?

Think about it ...

When you first heard about COVID-19 did you think it would have an impact on your life?

---

6 **to be hurting** to be affected in a negative way – 14 **to pretend** to act as if –
15 **whatsoever** at all

Chapter 4

Two months later, things were much worse. Now, Oscar had to hear a lot about the coronavirus. It was the only thing people talked about – the worldwide health emergency – the *pandemic*. There was also a name for the disease it caused: COVID-19. By the end of March, the U.S. led the world in cases – more than existed in China, Italy, Iran and other countries with high rates of infection.

The effects of COVID-19 varied a lot. Some people didn't feel very sick. Other people had mild symptoms: headache, cough, sore throat, fever, and body aches. Perhaps they lost their sense of taste or smell. Still others had severe symptoms: respiratory failure, rapid heartbeat, chest pains, high fever, and sepsis. Tragically, this led to thousands of fatalities around the world.

Because COVID-19 was highly contagious, people wore masks and gloves for protection. They were told to social distance, by keeping six feet away from others. Sporting events, concerts, and religious gatherings were cancelled. Schools closed. Offices closed. Even restaurants, like Oscar's, had to shut their doors.

Oscar worried about everyone affected by this illness. He heard that Linda – his regular customer – had been very ill with COVID-19. She couldn't leave her bed for two weeks. He heard that Linda's sister, Lena, was in the hospital with breathing problems. "She's in a *coma*," Mari said, wiping tears from her eyes. "She's on a *ventilator*," she added. "Lena might die… I mean… Can you imagine that?" Oscar shook his head sadly. He couldn't imagine it. It was like a bad dream.

After the restaurant closed, Oscar and Mari had to drive to Northern California. Without delay, they had to bring Clara back from school. It wasn't safe to be on a college campus. So,

---

3 **pandemic** a disease that affects people in many countries – 9 **symptom** physical signs that you have a disease – 10 **sore** painful – 10 **body aches** pain in your body – 11 **respiratory failure** a condition which means that there is not enough oxygen in the blood – 12 **sepsis** a life-threatening infection that can damage organs – 13 **fatality** death – 14 **contagious** easily passed from person to person – 23 **coma** a long state of unconsciousness – 24 **ventilator** a machine that helps people with a respiratory disease breathe

all students had to finish their classes online. Clara was very disappointed. She loved her school. She also had many friends and an active social life. Clara didn't want to move home. Yet, she had no other choice. The school year was over.

On the return trip, Oscar and Mari heard Clara blowing her nose in the back seat of the car. They knew she was unhappy. "Look, Clara," said Mari, tired of hearing her daughter cry. "It's a *pandemic*. People are *sick*. People are *dying*. You have to be reasonable." Clara grabbed a fresh tissue and dried her tears.

"Nobody likes this," added Oscar. "We have to do our part to control the spread of the disease. You study biology. Surely, you understand it."

"I do," said Clara weakly. "I'm just frustrated."

"So are we," said Mari. "Closing our business – the one that pays for your education – hurts us too."

"I know," Clara said. "I'm really sorry."

"Well," said Oscar, smiling for the first time all day, "there is *one* reason for you to feel better right now."

"What is it?" asked Clara, her voice sounding a bit stronger.

"While the restaurant is closed," said Oscar, "you won't have to wash dishes."

What is a pandemic?

What are the symptoms of a mild case of COVID-19?

Think about it ...

COVID-19 is very contagious. What should you do to avoid getting this, or any, infectious disease?

---

1 **frustrated** feeling upset because of an inability to do sth

Chapter 5

Oscar's was supposed to be closed for only two weeks. During that time, Oscar and Mari paid their employees: the cooks, the servers, the hosts, the bussers, the cashiers, and the dishwashers. They even paid the *mariachis*. The workers weren't responsible for the pandemic. Neither Oscar nor Mari wanted their staff to suffer financially. After all, the crisis would be over soon – they hoped.

Sadly, weeks passed, and dine-in restaurants, like Oscar's, still couldn't reopen. They had a take-out menu. But, not surprisingly, it wasn't very popular. In the past, people went to Oscar's for the experience. They liked the freshly served food and the festive atmosphere. Getting *enchiladas* in a to-go box wasn't the same. Besides, most customers were terrified of COVID-19. Perhaps a cook carried the virus. Or perhaps a cashier was infected. People

---

23 **to suffer** to be in a bad position – 27 **take-out** food you buy at a restaurant to eat at home

didn't want to get sick from contact with others. It wasn't worth it, even for "the best Mexican food in the world."

After several weeks passed, Mari and Oscar couldn't pay their employees anymore. With heavy hearts, they had to lay off most of their staff. As a result, some collected unemployment benefits. A few others found work elsewhere. A handful of employees went back to homes in Mexico. They couldn't live in Southern California without full-time jobs. This process was painful for Oscar and Mari too. They hated to see their workers scatter; some had worked at Oscar's since the first day. "I'll get in touch soon, Silvia," said Oscar, to his best server, his voice cracking with emotion. "I won't forget about you."

Oscar and Mari also felt a lot of financial pressure. They had their own bills: a home mortgage, a car payment, household expenses, and credit card debt. The restaurant earned almost no money right now. Yet, they still had to pay for utilities and building-maintenance costs, along with insurance and taxes. In the near future, they had to pay their daughters' school tuitions, even if they studied online. In addition, they supported Oscar's elderly mother in Mexico. It took a lot of money to take care of everyone and everything – money that was disappearing fast.

When business was good, it all worked like a well-oiled machine. And truthfully, Oscar and Mari loved supporting their employees. They loved supporting their family members too. Paying their bills used to be completely manageable – but not now. At present, it was impossible.

On a Friday evening, Oscar adjusted his facemask. Then he pulled a large sign onto the sidewalk in front of the restaurant. It read: WELCOME! WE'RE OPEN FOR TAKEOUT! But no one was there to pick up an order. The restaurant was

---

4 **to lay sb off** to tell sb they have to leave the company because there is no work – 5 **unemployment benefits** a payment made, usually by the government, to sb who has no job – 9 **to scatter** to separate and move in different directions – 16 **utilities** electricity, gas, water

unrecognizable – quiet and empty. Fourth Avenue, once lively with crowds, felt like a ghost town. Although Oscar's mouth was covered, Mari saw the sadness in his eyes. "It will get better," said Mari, joining Oscar on the deserted sidewalk. "Have faith."

"I'm trying to," said Oscar, sighing loudly.

"We need to stay positive, Oscar. Let's at least *pretend* that we're living the American dream," Mari said. Then, she squeezed his hand and returned inside the restaurant.

"With business like this," said Oscar, straightening the sign, "we're living the American nightmare."

> What were most customers afraid of?

> Why was Oscar finding it difficult to pay their bills?

Think about it...

How do you think Oscar felt when he had to lay off his staff?

Oscar was finding it difficult to stay positive. His wife helped him a lot. Who or what helps you stay positive when things are hard?

---

1 **unrecognizable** not familiar – 2 **ghost town** a town where no one lives – 4 **deserted** empty

Chapter 6

Oscar's restaurant wasn't the only business going down the drain. His neighbors on Fourth Avenue were hurting too: the hair salon, the health club, the movie theater, the nail salon and the hotel on the corner. Some places were completely closed. And some were just partially open, making a fraction of the revenue they once did. Most owners didn't know how much longer they could hang on.

One night, Majid, the hotel owner, came into Oscar's for a takeout dinner. "If things continue this way," he said, picking up his container, "I'll have to declare bankruptcy. I've run a successful business for twenty-five years… and now this."

"I can relate," Oscar said honestly. "These are terrible times. I'm losing my shirt." The situation in Southern California was frustrating, especially to shop owners. For them, it was like riding a roller coaster. For a while, the number of COVID-19 cases went

---

1 **to go down the drain** to be destroyed – 5 **revenue** money – 13 **to lose your shirt** to be in financial trouble

down. Then they went up again. Then down. Then up again. Controlling the general public was a problem. Not everyone obeyed the rules. Some people became careless. They gathered in large groups. They stopped wearing masks and spread infection.

One evening a young man marched into Oscar's. His face was completely uncovered. "Glad you're open," he said. "I'll take two fish tacos."

"Sorry," said Mari, speaking very seriously behind the plastic partition. "You're not allowed in here without a mask." The customer exhaled irritably. Mari stepped back. "It's the law," she added firmly. The young man pulled up his T-shirt to cover his mouth.

"Okay, now give me the two tacos," he ordered, pulling out his wallet.

"That's not a mask," Mari insisted. "I'm afraid that you'll have to leave." The young man was furious.

"This whole pandemic is a hoax!" he yelled, letting his T-shirt drop. "And people like *you* deserve to go out of business," he added, angrily walking out the front door.

"It's people like *him*," observed Fernando, their one cook, from the kitchen. "*They're* the reason we can't control the coronavirus. *They're* ruining it for everyone."

"Yes," agreed Mari, disgusted with the young man. But she was also disappointed that the restaurant had lost a sale – even a very small one.

*****

At last, in June, there was some great news. COVID-19 cases were steadily going down. Oscar's and other dine-in restaurants got the green light to reopen. Oscar and Mari were overjoyed. After a huge financial loss, they had hope again. Perhaps their business could be saved after all. Perhaps their lives could return to normal.

---

3 **to gather** to get together – 4 **to spread** to distribute – 10 **irritably** in a frustrated way – 16 **furious** very angry – 17 **hoax** sth that isn't true

In order to be safe, Oscar and Mari needed to make many changes. Inside the restaurant, furniture had to be removed and rearranged. There had to be more space between tables. There had to be fewer customers at one time. But *some* customers were definitely better than *no* customers. In addition, there were strict rules about sanitation and safety. There were no more shared menus. If employees had any symptoms of illness, they weren't allowed to work. And at work, everyone had to wear masks and gloves at all times.

Oscar got on the phone and immediately rehired ten of his best workers. He hoped to bring in the rest, including the *mariachis* later – when it was safe. Now, however, he had to be careful. It was early. The business wouldn't recover overnight. Silvia cried when she heard Oscar's voice on the phone. "Thank goodness I have my server job again!" she exclaimed. "What a relief!"

Why does Oscar compare owning a business to riding a roller coaster?

What changes do Mari and Oscar have to make to the restaurant?

Think about it ...

Mari refuses to sell food to a man who won't wear a mask. Do you think she is right? Why?

---

3 **to rearrange** to reorganize – 10 **to rehire** to hire sb after they have been laid off

Chapter 7

Oscar's and other restaurants were open for only two short weeks.
During that time, the number of COVID-19 cases went up. So,
restaurant owners had to close their dining rooms yet again.
Understandably, Oscar and Mari were devastated. It was all a waste
of money – rehiring workers, ordering supplies, and following new
regulations. The changes were for nothing. At that point, countless
restaurant owners gave up and shut their doors permanently.

Oscar nearly made the same decision. "The American dream
is over!" he announced, throwing his hands up in the air. "What's
left for us here?" he asked, sitting at the breakfast table with his
wife and daughters. "I'd happily wash dishes again at the Korean
restaurant – but they're out of business!"

25 **devastated** extremely upset – 28 **to shut their doors** to close

"Oh, Oscar. Please don't talk like that," said Mari. "Being pessimistic isn't going to help us. Think about what we *do* have: our health and a roof over our heads.

"Only until the house is in foreclosure," said Oscar angrily. "And then we'll be on the streets."

"That won't happen soon, Oscar," insisted Mari. "Many people are hurting right now. If we get behind on our mortgage, the lender must understand. It's the same with our other unpaid bills. A lot of Americans are in the same boat."

"Exactly," said Oscar. "That's why we're going back to *Mexico*!"

Recently, Oscar had begun to think about returning to his native country. He thought about the happier times there, when he was a child growing up. After all, he and his mother had lived in a beautiful part of the world: Cancún, on the Yucatán Peninsula. Tourists came from everywhere to visit Cancún, enjoying the turquoise sea and white sandy beaches.

The resorts were lovely, of course. They were places for people with a lot of money. His mother, however, worked in a hotel laundry room. It was windowless and hot. And beyond the hotel gates, life was not the same. By American standards, Oscar and his mother lived in poverty. Sometimes they had no electricity or running water.

At a young age, Oscar recognized the difference between the haves and the have-nots. So, when he was eighteen, he left Cancún. He didn't want to be stuck in a laundry room – or someplace worse – without any opportunity to get ahead. He bravely went after the American dream. And miraculously, after many years of hard work, his dream came true. He was very successful – until recently. Then the coronavirus undid everything and turned his life upside down.

Mari put down her fork and wiped her mouth. "Surely you've heard, Oscar. The pandemic is creating chaos in Mexico, too.

---

4 **to be in foreclosure** to take back a property after the owner doesn't make the monthly payment to the bank – 17 **resort** a place where people stay when they are on holiday – 24 **the haves** people who have things

There are thousands of COVID-19 cases and a high death toll – just like here. Besides, do you think restaurants in Mexico are making money right now? And our girls, well…"

"I won't move to Mexico, *Papi*," interrupted Clara. "There is no way that I can walk away from school, especially once it starts up again in person. If you and *Mami* can't help me with tuition, then I'll take out loans. Emma nodded her head in agreement.

"We love to visit *Abuela* in Mexico," added Emma. "It's wonderful there. Remember, though, you raised us in *this* country. The U.S. is our home. Clara and I have to stay here… with you… or without you."

> Why was Oscar's forced to close for a second time?

> Why did Oscar leave Mexico when he was younger?

Think about it …

How do you think Clara felt about the idea of moving back to Mexico? What do you think of the idea?

Many people make dangerous trips through Latin America to reach "El Norte" (the US). Why do you think they are prepared to take the risk?

---

1 **death toll** number of deaths – 5 **to walk away** to leave sth for no good reason –
8 **Abuela** (*Spanish*) grandmother – 9 **to raise** to take care a child until they are adult

Chapter 8

For the moment, Oscar and Mari kept the restaurant open. Their takeout business was tiny, compared to what they earned before the pandemic. But they decided not to give up completely. Meanwhile, their savings diminished and their debt grew. Using multiple credit cards, they paid some – but not all – of their home and business expenses. With apologies, Oscar sent his mother half the money he normally did. Unfortunately, other bills were simply impossible to pay, like their daughters' college tuitions.

Universities in the U.S. were expensive. In order to afford them, Clara and Emma had to borrow the money. They took out two types of loans: federal and private. Their parents were sad to see the girls go into debt. All this money had to be repaid someday – with interest. "Don't worry, *Papi*," said Clara, signing loan documents. "I'll have a good job after dental school – and this will be nothing."

"Don't be naïve," said Oscar, wringing his hands. "Paying for school will be a burden. You'll have this monkey on your back for years."

"They're doing what they have to do, Oscar," said Mari. "Let's not worry about this now. Our daughters need to focus on their academic goals."

"If business gets better, we'll help you again," promised Oscar.

"Not *if*…" said Mari firmly. "*When* business gets better, we'll help you again. This can't last forever. Eventually, we'll get back on our feet."

*****

In late August, Oscar and Mari got some encouraging news. They were permitted to reopen inside again. As before, they had to obey the strict seating and safety guidelines. Still, the business would make more money than it did with only takeout service.

---

2 **tiny** very small – 3 **to give up** to quit – 4 **to diminish** to became smaller – 13 **interest** extra money you have to pay the bank if they give you a loan – 16 **naïve** innocent – 17 **burden** a heavy load to carry – 24 **to get back on your feet** to be successful again – 28 **to obey** to behave, to do what sb tells you to do

This time, however, Oscar and Mari were less joyful. This had happened before. Perhaps they were on another roller coaster ride. They might open – then close again in a week or two.

On their first evening back, Oscar counted twenty-four people in the dining room. Six people waited patiently outside, spaced six feet apart on the sidewalk. Oscar was pleased to see them. "*Bienvenidas*!" he said, speaking to two masked women behind his own mask. "Welcome!" Then he pointed to the menu on a chalkboard hanging on the wall. "Our specials today are Yucatan-style chicken and onion stew… and…"

"Oscar," a woman laughed. "You haven't forgotten me, have you?" Oscar look confused. But then he recognized her voice. It was Linda, his regular customer for years. "And my sister, Lena, too," said Linda, indicating her companion. "You can see that we've recovered. Thank you and Mari so much for your calls – and thoughtfulness. Mari left soup on my doorstep multiple times. You people made me cry – in a good way!" Seeing Linda and Lena made Oscar feel emotional too.

"I'm so glad you're better!" said Oscar with heartfelt sincerity. "We worried about you both a lot. What an awful ordeal!"

"You have no idea," said Lena. "I was in the hospital for ten days, unable to breathe. It's a miracle that I survived."

"And it was no picnic for me either," said Linda. "I've never felt so sick in my entire life."

"I can't understand how some people think that the coronavirus isn't real," added Lena. "Believe us, it is!"

"Don't worry, though," insisted Linda. "That was five months ago. We're fine now. Our tests are negative. Our symptoms are gone. We're being very careful," she added, pointing to their masks. We just had to go to my favorite restaurant in the whole world. So happy you're open again!"

---

16 **thoughtfulness** consideration for other people's needs – 19 **glad** happy – 19 **heartfelt** honest – 22 **to breathe** to move air through your lungs

How did Clara and Emma pay for college when their parents could no longer help them?

How did Oscar and Mari support Linda and Lena when they were sick?

Think about it ...

In the US not everyone can afford to go to university because it is so expensive. Are universities more accessible in your country?

Do you think education should be free for everyone?

Chapter 9

It was wonderful to see customers inside Oscar's again. Yet it continued to be an uphill battle. Business was only thirty percent of what it was before. The restaurant couldn't possibly stay open – at that unprofitable level – for long. In order for Oscar's to exist, things had to improve very soon.

---

30 **to be an uphill battle** to be very difficult – 32 **unprofitable** making no money

Using the outdoor space was one way to serve more people. In an attempt to save their businesses, some restaurant owners had begun to serve customers on sidewalks and in parking lots. Fortunately, there was parking on the west side of Oscar's.

---

31 **sidewalk** the part of the pavement where pedestrians walk

Expansion was indeed possible, in the front and on the side, allowing for a new, L-shaped *al fresco* dining area.

Oscar and Mari liked the idea. Southern California had good weather; people were comfortable outside, especially in the summer. However, it was still risky financially. Making these changes required more money: outdoor tables, chairs, umbrellas, heaters, lights, and décor. The new areas needed to be securely fenced off. The parking lot had to be resurfaced – a big expense. Additional employees, tired of the roller coaster ride, had to decide whether or not to come back again. And after taking these costly steps, would enough customers return? Would the changes be worth the investment? For Oscar and Mari, it was a gamble.

Oscar didn't want to throw away any more money. "Let's think about this again after the girls go back to school. There is enough happening in our lives right now.

"Okay," said Mari. "But we should act quickly after that. Time is money."

*****

On two separate trips, Oscar and Mari took Clara and Emma to their schools. Clara returned to Northern California. Emma, a freshman, went to a school in Southern California, about two hours away. This semester, their classes were hybrid: some online and some in person. College campuses opened their dormitories again, but followed strict guidelines for sanitation and safety. Social distancing was required, and students had to wear masks when they were near other people.

As schools in the U.S. began to reopen, cases of COVID-19 exploded again. As with members of the general public, not all students obeyed the rules. They gathered unlawfully. They spread germs. And as a result, people in the school community – and beyond – got sick.

---

2 **al fresco** outdoors – 8 **fenced-off** separated by a fence – 9 **roller coaster ride** (*here*) unstable situation with ups and downs – 12 **gamble** risk – 13 **to throw away** to waste – 24 **guidelines** rules and recommendations – 29 **unlawfully** not allowed

These stories worried Oscar and Mari greatly. "Why do a few people have to ruin it for everyone?" complained Oscar, measuring the length and width of the sidewalk in front of the restaurant.

"It's shameful," said Mari, drawing a seating arrangement on a piece of paper. "And coming from students too. How can they be so smart and so foolish at the same time? They're endangering everyone!"

"It makes me really angry," said Oscar, retracting his tape measure with a snap. "Will we ever see an end to the coronavirus?

"Hopefully, they'll have a vaccine soon," said Mari. Just then, the phone rang in the pocket of her apron. It was Emma. "*Hola, Princesa*!" said Mari. "How are you?"

"I'm scared," Emma replied.

"What's wrong?" cried Mari, her heart pounding in her chest.

"Someone on my floor just tested positive for COVID-19," she said, her voice cracking with emotion. "So… I'm in quarantine."

How did Mari and Oscar decide to improve the business?

What kind of classes did Clara and Emma have?

---

5 **shameful** something that makes you feel angry and embarrassed – 7 **to endanger** to put sb in danger – 17 **quarantine** a period of time when sb is not allowed to have contact with other people to prevent the spread of a disease

They plan to convert the parking lot into a place to serve food. This is possible because the weather in California is good. Could this be done in your city?

As schools reopened in the US, more and more people gathered without following the guidelines. Do you think this was irresponsible? Why?

Chapter 10

Mari grabbed her heart and bit her lower lip. Then she put the call on speaker. "Are you feeling okay?" she asked.

"I'm feeling fine," said Emma. "But, you know, sometimes people have COVID-19 without symptoms. "I've just been tested… and I'm waiting for the results." This news was upsetting to both of her parents. Oscar looked up at the sky and let out a heavy sigh. "The girl with COVID-19 is pretty sick. They took her to another building. But as a precaution, the rest of us have to quarantine."

"For how long?" asked Oscar.

"For fourteen days," replied Emma. "And that's a *mandated* quarantine. That means we have to stay away from everyone,

---

28 **precaution** a measure taken to prevent a problem – 31 **mandated** obligatory

monitoring our symptoms." Emma explained that she had to check in with medical personnel every day. Instead of going to the main dining hall, she received meals at her door. "In my group," said Emma, "three other students were also exposed. I can see *them* – behind a mask – but I have no contact with anyone else."

"And you've only been in school for a few weeks. *Ay!* I wish I could bring you home," cried Mari.

"Me too, *Mami*," Emma responded tearfully. "But you can't. I'm not allowed to leave. And I can't spread germs to you and *Papi*."

That night, Oscar and Mari couldn't sleep. They felt bad for letting their daughters return to school. "I thought things were under control," said Oscar, unable to close his eyes. "How is this happening?"

"They obviously aren't under control, are they?" answered Mari, also tossing and turning in bed. "Nothing in the world feels under control right now," she added. "This illness worries me, Oscar. It worries me more than the business."

During the next two weeks, Oscar and Mari talked to Emma every day. Fortunately, her tests were negative. And she continued to feel well. The same was true with the other students in her group. No one had caught it. Fourteen days later, they were out of isolation.

Mari and Oscar also spoke to Clara regularly. Cases were reported on her campus too, but she hadn't been in contact – to her knowledge – with anyone who had it. But how could anyone be sure?

*****

"It feels like we're running around in circles sometimes," said Oscar, watching the workers pour fresh concrete onto their former parking lot.

"But we're not, Oscar," said Mari. "We're doing everything we can to protect our investment. Besides, it looks really nice out here," she added. "Just imagine the tables, the umbrellas, the lights, and some *papel picado* to brighten up the area. It will be beautiful." Mari waved to the workers with appreciation. "It will be smooth and level – much safer. We don't want anyone to fall down and get hurt."

"Right. And then sue us," said Oscar. "Just what we need: a lawsuit."

"Oscar," said Mari, "you really have to stop being so gloomy. It only makes things worse." Oscar looked down at his feet. "Do you remember washing dishes at the Korean restaurant? It wasn't fun – but you managed it. You did what you had to do, and the experience made you stronger. It made you dream big – it 'built character.' We will get through this, but let's… please… not make it harder than it already is."

> Why was Emma not allowed to see anyone?

> Why couldn't Oscar and Mari sleep?

Think about it…

> Emma is waiting for her test results. How do you think she is feeling?

> What are the positives and negatives of going into quarantine?

1 **papel picado** (*Spanish*) a Mexican decorative craft made by cutting designs into tissue paper – 2 **appreciation** thanks – 5 **to sue** to start a legal case against sb – 7 **gloomy** sad and negative

Chapter 11

In the middle of September, Mari, Oscar and three employees were busy organizing the outdoor dining areas. They positioned tables and chairs. They put up umbrellas and strung lights. They placed beautiful potted plants along the low fence that divided the new areas from the street. They even installed a fountain. Mari looked quite pleased. "A little higher, Enrique… please," she

advised one of the workers, as he stood on a ladder, pulling a long string of *papel picado* across the old parking area. "That's it," she said. "Perfect."

Just beyond the fence, a man walked by. "This place looks great!" he said, stopping in front. "Are you open for outside eating yet?"

---

29 **ladder** sth made of metal or wood with bars used to climb up or down sth

"We will be tonight," Mari replied. "Come and see us!"

"I'll do that," he promised. "Um, I used to eat at Oscar's once in a while… you know… before the…"

"Before the pandemic," interrupted Mari. "Yes, well, we're hoping our customers, like you, feel safer sitting outside *or inside* – at the appropriate distance, of course. We're following all the guidelines."

"For sure," said the man, waving good-bye. "I'll do that!" Oscar and Mari did everything they could to promote the restaurant. They made announcements on social media. They took advantage of the free advertising offered by a local radio station. By invitation, a TV reporter and cameraperson came to Oscar's. They did a story on the new expansion.

"This is lovely," said the reporter behind her mask. "I mean, I've eaten at Oscar's before. I know the food is incredible. But you've created a fabulous outdoor space here. It doesn't feel like a city sidewalk or a parking lot at all!"

"Thanks," said Mari. "Time will tell, of course. We're still dealing with a serious health crisis. And we don't expect people to throw caution to the wind," she added. "But we are doing everything in our power to protect our customers – and give them a great dining experience."

Just then, Oscar joined them. He dried his hands on his apron and bowed politely to her. "Thank you for coming," he said, making sure his mask covered his nose and mouth.

"It's my pleasure," said the reporter. "So," she began, "unlike many restaurants, Oscar's is still here. I'm guessing it's been very tough for you. How is it possible?"

"Mathematically," answered Oscar. "It doesn't work. And to stop the bleeding, so to speak, we needed to close weeks ago."

---

9 **to promote** to encourage sb to buy sth or support a cause – 24 **to bow** to bend forward as a sign of respect – 28 **tough** difficult – 30 **to stop the bleeding** to stop sth that causes a problem

"And what has made you carry on?" she asked, looking sympathetically at Oscar. At that question, Oscar felt a lump in his throat. Tears formed in his eyes. He couldn't speak.

"I think I can answer that," said Mari, wrapping her arm around Oscar's shoulder. "My husband doesn't quit, in spite of obstacles. He didn't achieve the success he had – before all of this – by chance. He did it through hard work and sacrifice. Did you notice that he was drying his hands when he joined us? That's because he's washing dishes again, like he did thirty years ago… as a new immigrant." Now Mari's voice began to break.

"It's like this," said Oscar, trying to contain his emotions." I want to help support my family and my employees – who are like my second family. I want them to be successful… like I was. I want them – *all* of them – to someday… live the American dream.

What did Mari and Oscar do to promote the restaurant?

Oscar says that he should have closed weeks ago. Why didn't he?

---

1 **to carry on** to continue – 2 **to feel a lump in your throat** to get a feeling in your throat when you're upset about sth

Think about it...

They hoped more customers would come
when they opened the outside area. Do you
normally prefer to eat indoors or outdoors?
And during the pandemic?

Mari says Oscar never quits. Even where
there are lot of obstacles. Do you think
this is positive or negative? Why?

Chapter 12

After two weeks, there was reason for optimism. In Mari's estimation, Oscar's was running at sixty-five percent of normal. Of course, it felt different from the old days. And customers never had to wait more than ten or fifteen minutes for a table. Still, the business no longer looked pathetic. There was life at Oscar's again. "It's contagious – in a good way," said Mari, smiling at Silvia. "When we look successful, we get more customers. No one wants to be on a sinking ship."

"Very true," said Silvia, carrying a tray of drinks to a large table outside. "I'm waiting on customers whom I haven't seen for months!" Mari wished that Oscar could see how busy it was today. But he was flying to Mexico.

"You absolutely have to go," insisted Mari the night before. "You're overdue to visit your mother – and she needs you now, after spraining her ankle."

"At least I can go for free, thanks to the credit card points," said Oscar. "That's one benefit to being in debt."

Oscar typically visited his mother about twice a year. He usually traveled with Mari, Clara, and Emma. But the girls were in school and Mari needed to watch over the business, especially now. Oscar's mother, Carmen, insisted that it wasn't an emergency. "These things happen," she said, discussing her recent injury. "My ankle isn't broken. I have crutches. I'm okay." Oscar refused to listen.

"I'll fly to Mérida tomorrow, Mamá," said Oscar firmly. "Mari can handle everything at the restaurant. I really want to see you."

Three years ago, after Carmen had retired from the hotel, she moved to Mérida, a city nearly two hundred miles from Cancún. She had good reasons for moving. First, Carmen wanted to be near her sister, nieces, and nephews in Mérida. Second, it was a less expensive place to live. So, Oscar helped her to rent a nice

8 **a sinking ship** (*here*) a business that is not going to survive – 14 **overdue** sth that was needed for a long time – 15 **to sprain** to twist – 23 **injury** physical damage – 23 **crutches** long sticks that people with a leg injury use to walk

apartment for seniors. "Look, Mamá!" said Oscar laughing. "It has electricity *and* running water!" Carmen laughed too. Thanks to Oscar, she'd also had those things many years ago. Nevertheless, her new home was the best place she'd ever lived.

Carmen's ankle was still bruised and swollen. Because she couldn't walk very far, she and Oscar spent a lot of time in her apartment. "I'll be honest with you, *Mamá*," said Oscar, helping Carmen to a chair. "It's been a horrendous year. The virus – it's hurt a lot of people physically and economically."

"I know," said Carmen. "A man in this building died of it three months ago," she said sadly. "Terrible."

"I'm so sorry that I've not been able to help you more," said Oscar, looking at his mother apologetically. "We have so many bills right now – our home… the girls' schools… the restaurant… the employees… it never ends."

"Please don't worry about me," said Carmen honestly. "I'm fine. You're a wonderful son – and I'm grateful to you and Mari."

"Well, we'll see what the future brings, *Mamá*," said Oscar, shrugging his shoulders. "Perhaps Mari and I will return to Mexico," he added. "If our business completely fails in the U.S., that's probably what we'll do.

"Try not to think about that right now," said his mother seriously. "It hasn't failed yet."

> How was business after two weeks of opening the outside area?

> Why did Oscar go to Mexico?

---

8 **horrendous** very bad – 19 **to shrug** to move your shoulders up and down very quickly to express uncertainty

Think about it...

Is it a good idea to travel during a pandemic? Why do people do it?

Do you agree with the advice Oscar's mother gave to him at the end of the chapter? Why?

Chapter 13

When Oscar returned from Mexico, he was relieved. The restaurant was still open. It wasn't making the money it once did, of course. But it wasn't closed. It felt like a victory. "Look at us," he said to Mari, laughing out loud. "We're celebrating just a thirty percent drop in business from last year!"

"Because it's better than being out of business," responded Mari, handing him a pair of rubber gloves. "There are a few pots and pans in the sink," she said with a smile. "Get busy!"

For Oscar, the hands-on work was therapeutic. There was no reason for him to stand around, counting customers. If business was slow, he worried. He preferred to be busy, even if that meant doing tasks that he hadn't done in years: preparing food, serving food, bussing tables, sweeping floors and, yes, washing dishes. It made him feel productive – and empowered.

28 **therapeutic** causing sb to feel better – 32 **to sweep** to brush away dirt

The employees enjoyed seeing Oscar roll up his sleeves and work next to them. He was their boss, but he worked hard too. In fact, he missed the morning staff meeting because he was chopping tomatoes and onions in the kitchen. "Mark my words," said Mari, speaking to the workers. "Oscar will be playing and singing with the *mariachis*… when it's safe for them to come back." Everyone laughed as Oscar entered the dining room.

"Did I miss something funny?" he asked.

"Not at all," said Silvia. "In fact, Oscar, I really appreciate your support when I'm serving. And you're doing very well. Just remember: You do most of the work. And I'll collect the tips."

Mari was right about success being contagious. As Oscar's sprang back to life, the rest of Fourth Avenue began to recover. They had been on the same roller coaster ride for months. At last, other businesses were improving too. The hair salon reopened. The health club partially reopened. The movie theater reopened, although their capacity was limited to twenty-five percent. And the nail salon reopened. Sadly, the hotel on the corner didn't survive.

It pained Oscar to see the big For Lease sign on Majid's building. His hotel had been a landmark in the neighborhood for years. "I had no choice," said Majid, sitting alone at a small table inside the restaurant. "I'd burned through all of my savings. I couldn't borrow any more money. At some point, I had to give up."

"It's not your fault," said Oscar. "You did everything you could. Who knew that a pandemic would affect our economy – not to mention our health – like this?" cried Oscar, adjusting his mask.

"And *my* staff," said Majid, picking up a paper napkin and drying his tears. "Like you, I employed a lot of people: clerks, maintenance people, housekeepers, and gardeners. Letting them

---

4 **to chop** to cut food into small pieces – 20 **for lease** for rent – 24 **to give up** to quit

go was awful. Majid took a drink from his water glass. Then Mari walked over to their table and brought Majid a large *tostada*.

"Your favorite," she said. "And it's on the house, Majid," she said. "We'll miss you a lot."

"Thanks," said Majid. "You've been such wonderful neighbors," he added. "And I'm really happy that you two survived this crisis."

"Well," said Oscar, "we're here today. But I've learned a very hard lesson: We can *never* be sure about tomorrow."

> Why was Oscar relieved when he got back from Mexico?

> What kind of boss is Oscar?

Think about it...

Oscar found doing the dishes therapeutic. What do you do to relax when you are stressed?

Mari says that success is contagious. Do you agree with her statement? Why?

---

2 **tostada** (*Spanish*) Mexican dish made with a toasted tortilla and a variety of toppings

Chapter 14

Clara didn't usually call her parents during lunch or dinner. The restaurant was busy at those times, and she didn't want to interrupt them. Still, she really wanted to talk to her father. Oscar felt the phone vibrate in his pocket. When he saw it was Clara, he quickly walked toward the exit door. "Are you okay?" he asked with concern.

"Yes, I'm fine, *Papi*," she said. "Why do you ask?"

"Because you're calling me now – when it's busy," he replied with some annoyance. "And we're in a pandemic. And I worry about you and your sister constantly… *That's* why I ask!"

"Oh, sorry," said Clara, trying not to laugh, even though irritating her father was a little funny. "Do I hear the *mariachis*?" she asked with surprise.

"Yes, you do," answered Oscar, sighing with relief that his daughter wasn't sick. "Is that why you're calling? Could you hear them from five hundred miles away? If so, then I'll ask them to be quieter." Clara laughed.

30 **to sigh** to make a loud sound when breathing

"They do sound a little quieter," observed Clara.

"That's because we have only two musicians for now," said Oscar. And they can't sing… because it spreads germs. But they can play their instruments and it's still beautiful."

"It's so nice to hear the music again, *Papi*! I wish I were at Oscar's tonight… even if I had to wash the dishes."

"That's my job now," said Oscar. "I think you need to focus on *your* career." Oscar signaled to Silvia that he was taking a five-minute break. "Well, you have my full attention now," he continued. "What's up?"

"Is the American dream a myth, *Papi*, or is it still attainable?" Clara asked.

"What do you mean by that?" asked Oscar.

"My professor claimed that it's much harder now – nearly impossible – for Americans to improve their quality of life. People who are born poor are going to stay poor. The social mobility you had, coming here with nothing and then becoming successful, is extremely rare. While it's a nice story – it's a story that isn't true today. Everything is different now."

Oscar took a deep breath and let it out slowly. He reflected on his own life experience. It's true that he came to the U.S. with practically nothing. It took him thirty years to become truly successful. Then he almost lost everything due to a pandemic. Now things looked a bit brighter. But they were definitely uncertain.

It was difficult for Oscar to answer Clara's question. What could he honestly say? Could Silvia *ever* hope to open her own restaurant someday – and be at the top of the ladder? Or was she stuck serving food forever, like his mother was stuck in a hotel laundry room? "I think that your professor is right. Things are different now. Everything is more expensive, and it is *much*

---

11 **attainable** sth that can be achieved – 18 **rare** not common – 28 **to be stuck** to be unable to move

harder. Maybe it is *rare* or *nearly impossible*. But to me… that *still* means *possible*."

"So you're saying," said Clara, "that the American dream is not a myth. You believe that anyone can succeed in this country, regardless of birthplace or class."

"Yes, I do," said Oscar. "In spite of all the obstacles, I really do. But believing it to be impossible – or *almost* impossible – is the wrong way to think. The American dream is definitely attainable – with very, very hard work… and ideally fewer pandemics. And learn from my mistake: a negative outlook is not constructive. Please tell your professor that I said so.

Why did Clara call her parents?

Why do they now only have two *mariachis* working in the restaurant?

Think about it …

Clara's university professor says that the American dream is now a myth not a reality. Do you agree? Why?

Oscar says that a negative outlook on life is never constructive. What do you think?

Chapter 15

20 In early October, Oscar had a birthday, his forty-ninth. He and
    Mari celebrated with a late dinner at the restaurant after it closed.
    The fall evenings had turned cool, so they sat near a heater on
    their beautiful *patio*, formerly the parking lot. "So much has
    happened since my last birthday," Oscar said, shaking his head.
25 "Can you believe what we've been through this year?"

      "We've weathered the storm so far," said Mari. "I'm quite proud
    of us," she continued, looking around the pretty outdoor area. "I
    love the sound of that fountain… and I just adore that giant bird
    of paradise behind you. It's magnificent, isn't it?" Oscar turned
30 around and admired the big plant with the colorful red, purple,
    and orange flowers.

---

26 **to weather the storm** to deal with a difficult situation successfully

"Yes, it's really nice out here," agreed Oscar. "And business isn't bad either. Eighty percent of what it was last year at this time. But under the circumstances, I'm very grateful."

"It's a miracle," said Mari. "Money is finally coming in. Most of our employees are back. We're paying… well… some of our bills. The girls are okay… although in a fair amount of debt." Mari shook her head and smiled. "But overall things are better than they were."

Silvia, wearing a mask, came out of the kitchen with two pieces of flan. She'd made it especially for Oscar's birthday. "*Feliz cumpleaños!*… Happy birthday!" she said putting two plates in front of them. "Sorry that your piece doesn't have any candles, Oscar. We can't have you blowing your germs everywhere." Both Oscar and Mari laughed.

"Definitely not," said Oscar. "The restaurant will close down again if I do that. But I'll still make a wish," he said, closing his eyes and pressing his hands together.

"What did you wish for?" asked Mari, as Silvia refilled their water glasses.

"I can't tell you," said Oscar with a wink. "I want it to come true." Indeed, Oscar had a real wish: an end to the pandemic. COVID-19 had wreaked havoc in the world, infecting millions and resulting in a staggering number of deaths. It had profoundly affected Oscar's life. It nearly ruined his livelihood – and hurt many people who were financially dependent on him.

Oscar would never, ever again believe that success was permanent. Living the American dream still required enormous effort – and a fair amount of luck. It was clear that things beyond Oscar's control, like the coronavirus, could destroy a person's dreams, sometimes irreparably – going from riches… to rags again. Fortunately, that hadn't happened. But who knew what

---

10 **flan** a Mexican dessert – 23 **staggering** shocking – 30 **from riches to rags** from rich to poor

the future would bring? For tonight, Oscar and Mari preferred to focus on more positive things: their family's good health and their triumph at remaining in business so far.

Silvia returned to their table to pick up their dessert plates. "My favorite dessert!" said Oscar. "Thank you so much!"

"Absolutely delicious!" exclaimed Mari. "No one makes flan like you!"

"You're very welcome," said Silvia. "It was my pleasure."

"You need to get home now," said Mari. "We can clean this up."

"Are you sure?" asked Silvia. "There are a few dishes back there and some pots and pans… and I can stay until…"

"Absolutely not!" said Oscar. "I'm happy to do them! You know, many years ago, when I was first learning English, I wrote some sentences in my notebook: 'Today, I *wash* dishes. Yesterday, I *washed* dishes.' Then, in the future tense, I wrote a negative one: 'Tomorrow, I *won't wash* dishes.' That's because washing dishes was a reminder that I was unsuccessful. However, I *will wash* dishes later tonight – and probably tomorrow too," he said, standing up and walking toward the kitchen. "And believe me, *big* dreams begin by scrubbing pots and pans. Like I've told my daughters many times, washing dishes is not only about survival. Even more importantly, it builds character."

What lesson has COVID-19 taught Oscar?

Why are pots and pans so important for Oscar?

---

2 **to focus** to concentrate

Think about it...

Oscar's birthday wish was to end COVID-19. If you could make a wish for the world, what would it be?

Oscar believes that effort and luck are key to being successful? Do you agree? What else is important?

Activities

Focus on the story

1. Are these sentences True or False?
Tick the correct box.

		True	False
1.	Oscar's is an Argentinian restaurant.	☐	☐
2.	As Oscar's English improved, he could find better jobs.	☐	☐
3.	Oscar has two daughters.	☐	☐
4.	Clara is Oscar's youngest daughter.	☐	☐
5.	Clara and Emma's universities were not too expensive.	☐	☐
6.	The new disease came from Wuhan, China.	☐	☐
7.	COVID-19 symptoms include headaches and fever.	☐	☐
8.	Oscar and Mari never laid off any of their employees.	☐	☐
9.	It was mandatory to wear a mask at Oscar's.	☐	☐
10.	Oscar managed to pay for Emma and Clara's university fees.	☐	☐
11.	Linda and Lena were very grateful to Oscar and Mari.	☐	☐
12.	Oscar and Mari decided to turn the restaurant's parking lot into a dining area.	☐	☐
13.	Emma tested positive for COVID-19 at her university.	☐	☐
14.	Oscar and Mari were happy with how the outside dining area looks.	☐	☐
15.	Oscar's attitude towards the future is still negative.	☐	☐

2. What happened when?

Put the events in the correct order. Put the correct letter next to the number.

a. A news reporter announced a lockdown in Wuhan, China.

b. Clara refused to move to Mexico.

c. The outdoor restaurant was generating profit and was a success.

d. COVID-19 cases went up because not all the students obeyed the rules.

e. Majid's hotel closed.

f. The waiting time for a table at Oscar's is one hour.

g. Oscar's was forced to close.

h. Oscar and Mari used their credit cards to pay the bills.

i. Emma is in her last semester of high school.

j. Oscar and Mari decided to use the outdoor space to serve customers.

1. _____

2. _____
3. _____

4. _____

5. _____
6. _____

7. _____
8. _____

9. _____
10. _____

3. What happened where?

Match the place to what happened there.

1. a Korean restaurant
2. Oscar's restaurant
3. Majid's hotel
4. Merida, Mexico
5. Emma's university

a. Someone tested positive for COVID-19 and everyone had to go into quarantine.
b. It was closed due to COVID-19.
c. Oscar visited his mother.
d. Clara and Emma worked there.
e. Oscar worked as a dishwasher.

1	2	3	4	5

4. How did you like it?

Reflect on the story and complete the review form.

What I liked

1.

2.

3.

What I didn't like

1.

2.

3.

My favorite character is _____ because:

My favorite chapter is _____ because:

Stars: _____ / 5

☆☆☆☆☆

Focus on the people

1. Were you right?

Go back to the **Before you start** section of the book. Look back at the adjectives you chose to describe the characters. Were you right? Add the adjectives you would now choose to the table below.

a. Oscar	**b. Mari**	**c. Clara**	**d. Emma**

2. Who did what?

Read the sentences and decide which character above did what.

1. _____ didn't serve a customer because he wasn't wearing a mask.
2. _____ worked at a Korean Restaurant as a dishwasher.
3. _____ has just started university.
4. _____ didn't want to move to Mexico.
5. _____ was quarantined at the university.
6. _____ left soup for Linda and Lena on their doorstep.
7. _____ went to Merida to visit a relative.
8. _____ called asking if the American dream was over.

Focus on grammar

1. Which word fits best?

Write the time connector that best fits the gaps. You can use the words more than once.

when	while	as soon as	before	after	until

1. Oscar was very successful _____ recently.
2. _____ the restaurant is closed, Clara won't have to wash dishes.
3. Oscar and Mari re-opened their restaurant _____ they could.
4. Oscar and Mari were worried that _____ all the costly steps, the restaurant wouldn't recover.
5. Silvia cried _____ she heard Oscar's voice on the phone.
6. They were earning less money than _____ the pandemic.
7. Oscar went to Mexico _____ he heard his mother was injured.
8. Oscar and Mari's restaurant remained closed _____ they were allowed to open again.
9. _____ Oscar returned from Mexico he was happy to see the restaurant was still open.
10. _____ working in restaurants for more than 20 years, he knows the business really well.

2. Past simple or past perfect?
Choose the right form of the verb.

1. Oscar **had worked/worked** in many restaurants before he decided to open his own.
2. Mari **had decided/decided** to rebuild the parking lot to fit more customers.
3. After 14 days, no one at Emma's university **had caught/caught** the virus.
4. Before the pandemic, the restaurant **had never been/never was** in such danger of closing.
5. Before the local hotel closed, it **had been/was** a landmark for years.

3. What are the COVID-19 safety measures?
Look at the COVID-19 rules below and complete the sentences on the next page with a modal verb (e.g. will, won't, mustn't, should). Add two of your own rules.

COVID-19 SAFETY MEASURES
[set of 10 important do's and don'ts]

Wash Hands Thoroughly

Use Soap or Hand Sanitizer

Keep Safe Distance from Other People

Stay at Home if Possible

Use Face Mask or Respirator

Avoid Large Crowds

Do Not Meet Infected or Sick People

Do Not Touch Your Face esp. Mouth, Eyes, Nose

Do Not Travel Unless Necessary

Do Not Touch The Front Part of a Mask

1. You _____ use public transport. If you _____, it is safer to go in a car.

2. You _____ go in a shop if you aren't wearing a mask.

3. You _____ always wash your hands when you use the bathroom.

4. You _____ to use soap when you wash your hands. You _____ sanitize them as well.

5. You _____ join the class online or you _____ go to school, but you _____ wear a mask and the teacher _____ open the windows for 10 minutes every 20 minutes.

6. You _____ drink out of the same bottle as anybody else.

7. You _____ _____.

8. You _____ _____.

Build your vocabulary

Focus on words

1. What's the word?

Unscramble the words so that they make a word about health.

urnqineata		a period of time when sb is not allowed to have contact with other people to prevent the spread of a disease
rehbeat		to move air through your lungs
psmytsom		the physical signs that show that you may have a disease
deeasis		an illness
ogocsaitun		when a disease is passed from person to person quickly
anipmecd		a disease that affects a whole country, or the world
ijynru		physical damage usually caused by an accident
kloocndw		when the government decides to close everything e.g. schools and shops, and limit people's movement
adnecist		standing 6ft. / 2m away from other people
nsraeiitz		sth you can use to make your hands even cleaner than normal

2. Which word fits best?

Fill in the gaps using a word from the previous exercise.

1. I _____ my knee playing football.

2. If you're stressed, it's important to be mindful and
   _____.

3. To help prevent the spread of the _____ people need
   to respect social distancing rules.

4. Coughing, and fever are common _____ of the flu.

5. If you have a _____ illness, it's best to stay at home.

A Viral Disturbance – the mind map

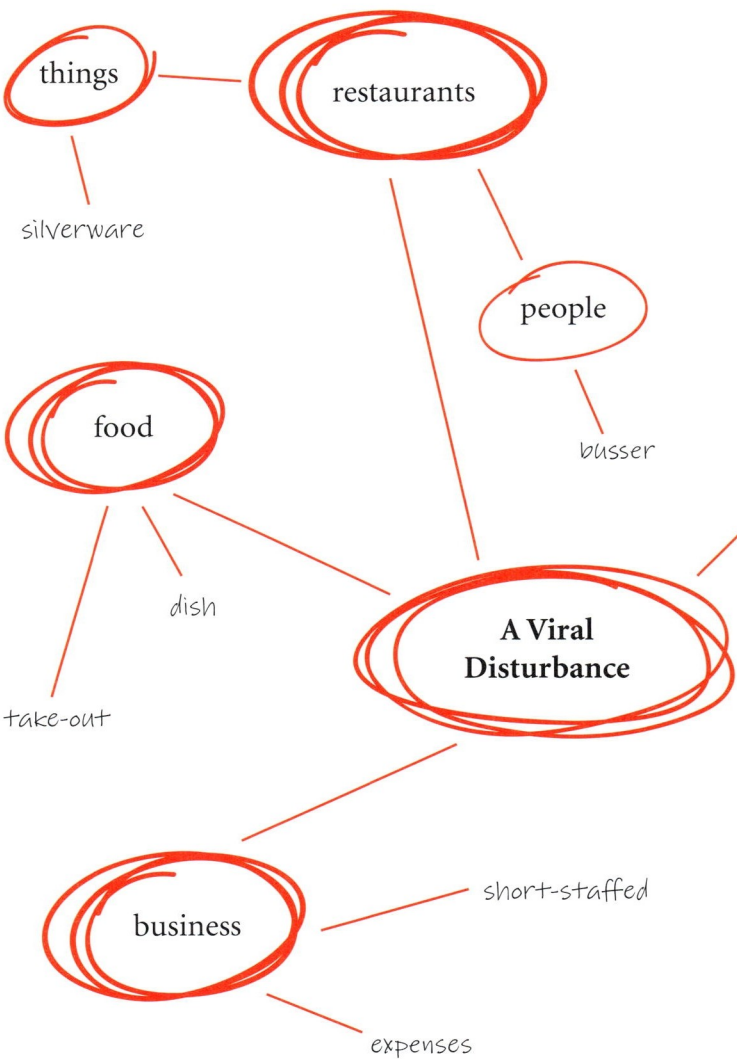

things

restaurants

silverware

people

busser

food

dish

take-out

A Viral Disturbance

business

short-staffed

expenses

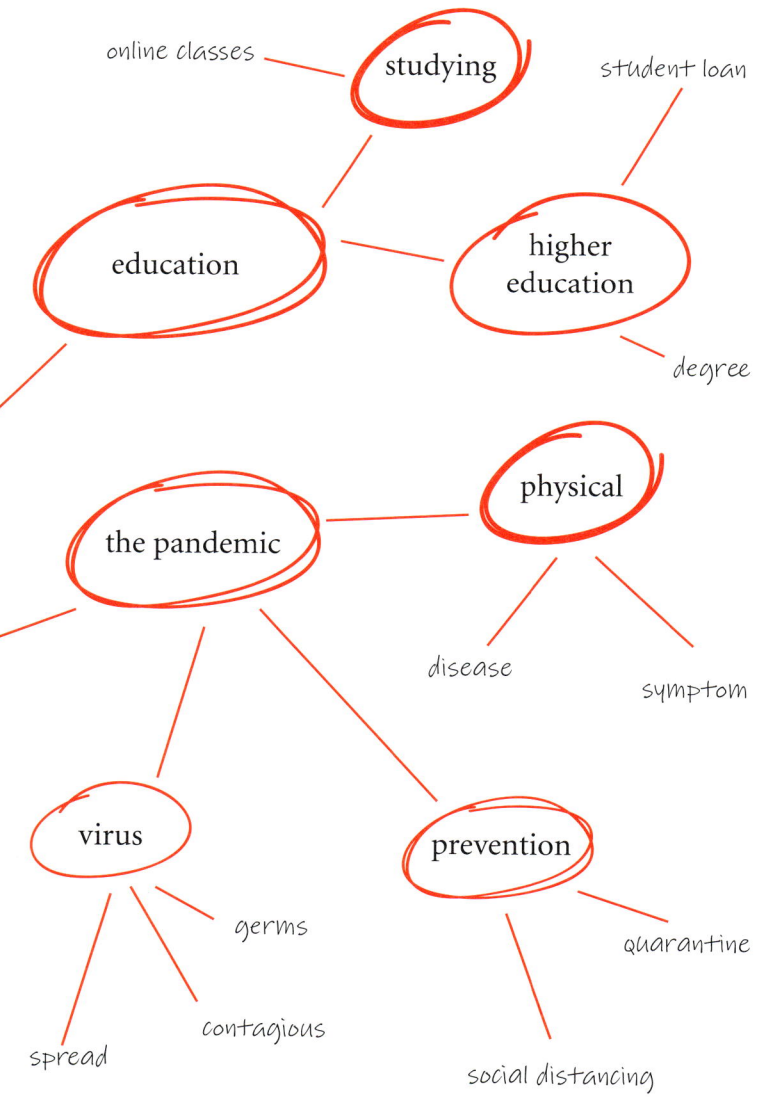

online classes — studying — student loan

education — higher education — degree

the pandemic — physical — disease — symptom

virus — germs — contagious — spread

prevention — quarantine — social distancing

Glossary

	New word?	Notes / connected words
Education		
college campus	☐	
degree	☐	the certificate you receive at the end of your studies
dormitory	☐	
freshman	☐	
online classes	☐	
semester	☐	
student loan	☐	
tuition	☐	
university	☐	
The pandemic		
aches	☐	
be infected	☐	
cancellations	☐	
carry a virus	☐	
contagious	☐	
disease	☐	
fatalities	☐	
germs	☐	
isolation	☐	
lockdown	☐	
mask	☐	
quarantine	☐	
sanitation	☐	
social distancing	☐	
spread	☐	
sore	☐	
symptom	☐	
test positive / negative	☐	

	New word?	Notes / connected words
Restaurants		
busser	☐	
cook	☐	
customer	☐	
follow regulations	☐	
kitchen	☐	
menu	☐	
order supplies	☐	
outdoor tables	☐	
patron	☐	
placemat	☐	
serve	☐	
silverware	☐	
Food		
dish	☐	
flan	☐	
take-out	☐	
stew	☐	
tacos	☐	
tostada	☐	
Business		
borrow	☐	
drop in business	☐	
earn	☐	
expense	☐	
foreclosure	☐	
hire	☐	
insurance	☐	
lay sb off	☐	

Find out more

Staying positive

1. The coronavirus pandemic has caused many problems around the world, however, as Oscar said, it's important to stay positive. Think of 10 positive things we can do in order to make the world a better place.

1.

2.

3.

4.

5.

6.

7.

8.

9.

10.

Make a poster

2. Make a poster with 10 guidelines to prevent the spread of common diseases.

Answer key

Focus on the story – questions at the end of each chapter

Chapter 1
- Suggested answers: a success, busy, crowded, full, popular
- For over 20 years he worked very hard and climbed his way up the ladder at several different restaurants. The bank then gave him a loan to start his own restaurant.

Chapter 2
- As their lives are quite privileged, Oscar believes doing jobs like washing dishes will help them understand how important it is to be prepared to do any job and that doing things they don't want to do will help build character.
- She needs to get the germs off her hands as she has been touching used glasses and napkins.

Chapter 3
- She wanted to make sure that the virus stayed out of the restaurant.
- He was worried about the virus even if it was mostly on the other side of the ocean at the moment.

Chapter 4
- A pandemic is a worldwide health emergency like an infectious disease that spreads quickly.
- The examples given here are: headache, cough, sore throat, fever, and body aches.

Chapter 5
- They were afraid of catching the virus.
- The customers weren't coming anymore and with no income he had to pay his staff.

Chapter 6
- There are lots of ups and downs and you don't know what's coming next.
- They have to take some furniture out and rearrange the tables and chairs so that there is enough space between people. They have to follow strict hygiene rules, make sure that there are more menus so people don't share them, and wear masks and gloves all the time.

Chapter 7
- The cases went up again and no-one was coming to the restaurant. Oscar couldn't afford to keep it open.
- He didn't want to live a life of poverty like his mother. He wanted a future full of opportunities.

Chapter 8
- They took out loans which they will pay back once they have graduated and are working.
- Oscar and Mari helped them while they were so ill.

Chapter 9
- They decided to convert the parking lot into a dining area.
- Their classes were hybrid: some online and some in person.

Chapter 10
- She has to go into quarantine.
- They feel bad about letting their daughters return to school.

Chapter 11
- They made announcements on social media and took advantage of free advertising on a local radio station.
- He doesn't quit even when things are tough.

Chapter 12

- It was getting better and was at about 65% of normal.
- To visit his mother because he normally does this about twice a year, she lives on her own and he wants to spend time with her.

Chapter 13

- The restaurant was open and they were at least making some money.
- He is very hands-on and likes to work with his employees.

Chapter 14

- To talk to them about the wider consequences of the pandemic – like the American dream being over.
- They can't sing as this may spread germs. They can play instruments though. They therefore don't need so many.

Chapter 15

- That you shouldn't believe that success is permanent. Anything unexpected can take it away.
- Big dreams begin by scrubbing pots and pans.

1. 1. F, 2. T, 3. T, 4. F, 5. T, 6. T, 7. T, 8. F, 9., 10., 11. T, 12. T, 13. F, 14. T, 15. F
2. 1. f, 2. i, 3. a, 4. g, 5. b, 6. h, 7. j, 8. d, 9. e, 10. c
3. 1. e, 2. d, 3. b, 4. c, 5. a

Focus on the people

2. 1. Mari, 2. Oscar, 3. Clara, 4. Emma and Clara, 5. Emma, 6. Mari, 7. Oscar, 8. Clara

Focus on grammar

1. 1. until, 2. While, 3. as soon as, 4. after, 5. when, 6. before, 7. as soon as, 8. until, 9. When, 10. After
2. 1. had worked, 2. decided, 3. caught, 4. had never been, 5. it had been
3. (Suggested answers) 1. shouldn't / can, 2. mustn't, 3. must, should, 4. have, need / should, must, 5. can / can / have to, must, need to / should, needs to, has to, 6. mustn't

Focus on words

1.

quarantine	a period of time when sb is not allowed to have contact with other people to prevent the spread of a disease
breathe	to move air through your lungs
symptoms	the physical feeling that indicates that you have a disease
disease	an illness
contagious	when a disease is passed from person to person quickly
pandemic	a disease that affects a whole country, or the world
injury	physical damage usually caused by an accident

lockdown	when the government decides to close everything e.g. schools and shops, and limit people's movement
distance	standing 6ft. / 2m away from other people
sanitizer	sth you can use to make your hands even cleaner than normal

2. 1. injured, 2. breathe, 3. disease, 4. symptoms, 5. contagious